Praise for
Dare to Care in the Workplace and Kathleen Quinn Votaw

"Adapting to our new normal post-pandemic poses a challenge for today's business leaders. Guidance from Kathleen Quinn Votaw arrives at a perfect time to ease you through this transition period and get you on the right path to lead your team to new heights. This is a must-read."

—MONICA SMILEY
Editor and publisher, Enterprising Women

"Don't forget everything you learned in business school about how to lead, but do add to your arsenal of skills that you have to have in this latest era of changes in the workplace. How do you do that? Kathleen Quinn Votaw gives us a recipe book that applies to a start-up of six people as well as an organization employing thousands. Trust, hope, listening, and really, really focusing on our employees with the same energy we have historically done with our customers are our new norms. Bring a pencil when you open this book. You will want to make sure you highlight her lessons while you create your company Camelot."

—JOHN KELLEY
Chairman and executive director, CereHealth

"In *Dare to Care in the Workplace*, Kathleen Quinn Votaw serves as your guide to navigate uncertainty and continuous change. Amidst all of the chaos, leaders who rely on guiding principles while committing to respecting the individual can look ahead and see a year filled with ongoing learning, improved collaboration, better results, and even the potential of reaching the Camelot Community!"

—SAM REESE
CEO, Vistage Worldwide, Inc.

"Once again, Kathleen nails the current realities of work with forthright, heart-centered wisdom. Leaders who pay attention to the new expectations for purpose, trust, and caring in our workplaces will have the edge as we face a renewed war for talent in the post-pandemic era. Kathleen provides a simple guide to helping those leaders get there."

—LORI GILLEN FRASIER
Chief human resources officer, CPI Card Group

"Leading a team in turbulent and changing times is difficult. *Dare to Care in the Workplace* is a refreshingly easy guide on how to do it well. This is a must-read for any manager."

—ADAM WITTY

Founder and CEO, Advantage|ForbesBooks

"Leading, managing, inspiring, and holding yourself and others accountable are the hardest things in business, and the pandemic just made them harder. As leaders and managers, we need help to find our way through these unprecedented times. Kathleen Quinn Votaw's book is an essential guide and a great resource that we all need. Thank goodness!"

—MARK HEMMETER

Founder and CEO, Office Evolution

"Having worked with Kathleen early in my career, this book epitomizes the culture she created—empathetic, caring, and high performing. This book takes these lessons and helps us lead with care."

—SCOTT RAGUSA

President, Planet Technology and Planet Professional

"The best companies know what it means to put their people first, and every other business is left to figure out what that means in order to compete. With *Dare to Care in the Workplace*, Kathleen Quinn Votaw offers leaders an essential and heartfelt guide to creating what she calls Camelot Communities that attract and retain top talent. They're based on cultures where listening, trust, inclusiveness, empathy, respect, and kindness prevail—and judging others is nowhere in sight. You may see yourself in these pages."

—MICHAEL BUSH
CEO, Great Place to Work US

"Kathleen Quinn Votaw puts a new spin on the 'employee first and the rest will follow' mindset that most of us, as business owners, try to achieve. This has become even more difficult during the COVID-19 pandemic when many of us struggled with even the simplest of business strategies. Kathleen's book is an easy read that reminds us of how important culture and a (mentally) healthy workspace are during these uncertain times. *Dare to Care in the Workplace* helps business owners answer some of the most important questions that have emerged over the past year: What does a hybrid or work-from-home environment look like at my company? How can I trust my employees to be productive at home? Do I show enough empathy when addressing my employees' personal challenges? An absolute must-read for any business owner trying to create a new normal."

—AMI KASSAR
Multifunding founder and CEO
Author, The Growth Dilemma
Speaker
Contributor to Inc., *EO, and YPO communities*

"Our workplace has changed! Companies are planning for what is ahead with new working models. They realize this will be a roller coaster ride as they determine the right model for their organization. But the most important part of all of this change is the *human* side. In *Dare to Care in the Workplace*, Kathleen Quinn Votaw helps leaders understand and navigate how to lead and communicate with respect for others first. This book is the road map to putting people first and will help you create your unique Camelot Community."

—YOLANDA HARRIS
CEO, The Keynote Group

DARE
to CARE
—— IN THE ——
WORKPLACE

Kathleen Quinn Votaw

DARE
to CARE
— IN THE —
WORKPLACE

A Guide to the New Way We Work

Advantage®

Published by Advantage, Charleston, South Carolina.
Member of Advantage Media Group.

ADVANTAGE is a registered trademark, and the Advantage colophon is a trademark of Advantage Media Group, Inc.

Printed in the United States of America.

10 9 8 7 6 5 4 3 2 1

ISBN: 978-1-64225-289-7
LCCN: 2021912705

Cover design by Mary Hamilton.

This publication is designed to provide accurate and authoritative information in regard to the subject matter covered. It is sold with the understanding that the publisher is not engaged in rendering legal, accounting, or other professional services. If legal advice or other expert assistance is required, the services of a competent professional person should be sought.

 Advantage Media Group is proud to be a part of the Tree Neutral® program. Tree Neutral offsets the number of trees consumed in the production and printing of this book by taking proactive steps such as planting trees in direct proportion to the number of trees used to print books. To learn more about Tree Neutral, please visit **www.treeneutral.com**.

Advantage Media Group is a publisher of business, self-improvement, and professional development books and online learning. We help entrepreneurs, business leaders, and professionals share their Stories, Passion, and Knowledge to help others Learn & Grow. Do you have a manuscript or book idea that you would like us to consider for publishing? Please visit **advantagefamily.com** or call **1.866.775.1696**.

To my husband, Andy Votaw—
my life, my love, and my favorite hobby. :)
Thank you for believing in me.

CONTENTS

AUTHOR'S NOTE

You can never really know what another person is thinking or feeling. We are essentially solitary creatures. This is one of the "whys" behind *Dare to Care in the Workplace* as we seek to find ways to understand others' perspectives.

My point is that if we do not reach out as leaders, human nature will kick in and others won't dare to share with us unless invited. This is because of the traditional hierarchy separating employer and employee—you know, the way things have always been. We must finally create a new reality of selfless communication that puts people first and act on the age-old phrase, "people are your most important asset."

This book was written during the early recovery from the pandemic. At the time of publication, we are largely back to business and school—but in new ways.

Both workplaces and leadership have forever changed, and all the skills that applied throughout our recovery will apply long into the future.

INTRODUCTION

The 2020 COVID-19 pandemic forever changed the way we work. A bit like Meriwether Lewis, William Clark, and Sacagawea, we are pioneers. We are navigating this new world of working from home—or what I like to call working from anywhere (WFA). On this journey, we do not always know where we are going or what we will find, and we are likely to get lost from time to time.

THE SIMPLE THINGS

At the time of writing this book, we are in the second year of the COVID-19 pandemic. We have experienced a lifetime's worth of uncertainty with various states of change, fluctuating rules, and individual comfort levels, making even the simple things like how we greet one another challenging.

A friendly handshake? A playful bumping of elbows? Now out of bounds. They require a touch. Is waving okay? How long do we need to hide our faces behind masks? That is just the tip of the uncertainty we continue to face.

I am not certain that anyone actually thrives in this environment, but I do see many people in conflict over seemingly small things and the elevated stress often leads to anger. We need to help our employees by modeling and leading with kindness, empathy, and understanding—never judgment.

> **We need to help our employees by modeling and leading with kindness, empathy, and understanding— never judgment.**

JUDGMENT TRAP

If there's an overall theme for the pandemic, it is judgment. Retrieving our balance and figuring out how to eliminate this destructive form of relating will be tricky. We have people who are returning to work in the office, those who are still working remotely, and over 70 percent of employers now planning to offer a hybrid form of working.[1] This means that even in routine meetings people may choose to join in person, via audio, or on video. When we are characters on a screen, losing sight of the real people behind the screen is easy.

A case in point: In my recent weekly team meeting, I had nine people attending in person and six participating virtually. One of my employees contacted me before the meeting and asked, "Why the hell isn't everyone coming in person?" Different comfort level, different preferences. That is where the judgment sets in.

It is hard for us not to judge. But we have to learn to say, "That is good for you; it might not be okay for me, but I care about you and respect your choices." Life at work is going to be different just as life at home and in social settings is different. All of us need to work together, leaders and employees, to figure out how to eliminate judgment from our culture and create a workplace based on empathy, respect, trust, and transparency.

---

1   Nicholas Bloom, "Don't Let Employees Pick Their WFH Days," *Harvard Business Review*, May 25, 2021, https://hbr.org/2021/05/dont-let-employees-pick-their-wfh-days.

AIM FOR CAMELOT

Reaching that sweet spot can lead to what I call a "Camelot Community." Imagine employees who work for you as part of following their life's calling—not clocking in and out for just a paycheck but excited and motivated to be there. Their passion manifests in what they do, how they do it, and the experience they create for your customers.

The Camelot Community is rare. It grows from the hard work of managing people with patience and persistence over time, creating a multitude of Camelot "moments" that allow you to feel something special is growing. The employee experience from Camelot moments isn't a task to check off your to-do list; it is a goal worth pursuing.

This is what this book is all about: Putting people first and focusing on the employee experience as much as you focus on the customer experience, leading you directly to the sweet spot of success—your unique Camelot.

MY PERSPECTIVE

The challenges and uncertainties we face make it easy to go back to the way it was. Our old work practices are associated with "normal," and it is easier to go back to the status quo. Sadly, that is what I am seeing happen in workplaces everywhere. "Let's bring everyone back to the office and be 'normal' again" isn't possible—or desirable.

The fact is that workplaces have been changing for several years, driven early on by millennials and gen Z who demanded more inclusive and motivating work environments. Then all six working generations joined them in wanting more purpose, work/life balance, flexibility, and inclusion from employers. People now expect empathy and transparency from their leaders; they want leaders who show they care about them as human beings.

This is where we are, and leaders who dare to change the status quo are doing the right thing for their employees and their business. Yes, change is hard, but it also creates unimagined opportunity. Grab the moment. *Dare to Care in the Workplace* is meant to serve as your guide.

Never one to talk and not act, I offer my firm, TalenTrust, as an example of what's to come. We have been operating in a hybrid setting since 2003 with employees all over the United States. I've built my business, and guided others, on a foundation of kindness and love. We have succeeded and failed together over the years, and what I have learned is that when you put your people first, good things happen.

To date, we have helped more than one thousand companies across multiple industries navigate uncertainty and continuous change. These companies have developed purpose-based cultures, targeted powerful recruitment strategies, and most importantly, inspired employees who want to come to work every day. They are striving for that Camelot Community, where people are appreciated and supported as the most valuable assets and leaders lead with empathy and dare to care. When you reach Camelot, the employee experience directly flows to your customers' experience. My goal with this book is to help you get there.

Key Takeaways

It takes everyone at a company working together to create a supportive employee experience. As you read this book, take time to reflect on how your role fits into this new dynamic. Do not just read. Think. Ask questions. Take action.

When you have finished reading this book, you'll have actionable ideas on:

- Leading with respect

- Modeling and fostering transparency

- Using empathy to enhance employee experience

- Creating a Camelot Community that inspires, motivates, and supports your employees

CHAPTER 1

HAVE A LITTLE FAITH IN ME

I believe in people, process and products, but people are the most important thing.

—MARCUS LEMONIS

Every generation has survived something remarkable. Within my life span, we have endured wars, terrorism, natural disasters, and now a pandemic. The way we work together has forever changed after the events of 2020. We have survived extraordinary times, and we are all trying our best in this new space. Everything from the handshake to the video call is awkward.

CEOs and employees alike are trying to figure out how we show up at work.

- How do we connect with people in this new workplace?

- How do we navigate remote and hybrid spaces?

- What are the social norms for video calls? Hybrid calls?

- What do we wear?

- What does my video background need to look like?

- Can we eat, drink, or walk during a video meeting?

- Are we going to be forgotten if we are not in the office with hybrid or on-site workers?

- Will people lose opportunities for advancement if they do not come to work in person?

- How can I lead a hybrid team?

Navigating the new hybrid work environment is complicated by having multiple groups participating in different ways. First, we have customers who may be remote, in person, or hybrid. Second, we have employees who are remote, in person, or hybrid. Same issues to handle but too often the sole focus is on serving the customer, and the employee experience is brushed aside. This leaves your employees high and dry and without proper support in our world of stress and unrest. This is not only bad practice but also a recipe for failure. Supporting employees and keeping them happy greatly increases your ability to retain top talent and ensure a positive customer experience that leads to company growth.

Invest in your employees and they will invest in you. As employers, we must remember that we are not just hiring someone with a certain skill set; we are hiring the whole person. To move forward in addressing the range of traits, experiences, and needs each person brings with them to the workplace, we need to lead with faith in our people and copious amounts of love, trust, and kindness. Having faith in your employees involves creating a community of respect, trust, transparency, and a touch of fun. Sounds idealistic, but you can make it happen.

> **To move forward in addressing the range of traits, experiences, and needs each person brings with them to the workplace, we need to lead with faith in our people and copious amounts of love, trust, and kindness.**

CH-CH-CHANGES

Shifting from on-site to remote or hybrid settings poses a whole new set of social norms and workplace dynamics, from daily responsibilities to customer interactions. Companies need to adapt or risk falling off the radar of current and future customers *and* prospective talent. In fact, 52 percent of employees are planning to look for a new job in 2021—a concerning 43 percent increase from 2020 and 2019.[2]

Change makes people nervous and afraid. Companies with a long history, and those that employ significant numbers of older generations, tend to have bigger problems with change and a preference for trying to maintain the status quo. Our workplaces are more diverse now than ever in the past, in terms of generations, gender differences, and ethnicities. We have to give everyone, including ourselves, time to adapt to the enormous change that is coming at us from every direction and have faith that we can not only handle it but will benefit from it.

---

2   Achievers, "Engagement and Retention Report 2021," March 2021, https://www.achievers.com/wp-content/uploads/2021/03/Achievers-Workforce-Institute-2021-Engagement-and-Retention-Report.pdf.

There are several ways to incorporate faith into your workplace culture:

- Lead with respect

- Communicate effectively

- Build trust

- Break the mold

- Make it all fun

I am thinking of a client of mine from Ohio, "Mr. Jones," who struggled with the transition to more remote workspaces. One of Mr. Jones's top salespeople was out walking their dog when they took a sales call. Mr. Jones was furious. He said to me, "Oh my God—I cannot believe this employee would take a call while he's outside walking the dog!" What happened here? Was the salesperson in the wrong? Was there a hidden reason behind Mr. Jones's response? Let's dive into leading with respect and see how having a little faith can make a big difference. We will circle back to Mr. Jones later in this chapter.

LEAD WITH RESPECT

There's a lot of misunderstanding and broken communication going on in the wake of the upheaval in our lives from the COVID-19 pandemic. Uncertainty can lead to frustration and frustration too often leads to anger. The reality is that we are all feeling the emotional impact of change.

While we cannot control what happens to us, we do have control over our reactions. As leaders and employees, we need to have faith in each other and work together to build trust that helps us overcome the challenges and negativity that come our way. We must react from a place of positive intent, not in the heat of the moment when emotions are flying high.

> **As leaders and employees, we need to have faith in each other and work together to build trust that helps us overcome the challenges and negativity that come our way.**

Let's be honest here, disagreements happen even when we are all working cooperatively and with respect. It is helpful to keep in mind that differences of opinion are not necessarily bad; they can shed light on pain points such as unfairness, or policies that may need updating, and lead to innovation. Circle back to the need to lead together: Leadership based on mutual respect makes a better workplace and better people within it.

COMMUNICATE EFFECTIVELY

The key to successful communication and change is having a little faith. We are talking here about faith in terms of trust, loyalty, and creating psychological safety. The steps to having faith in others are:

- Listen first, always

- Understand what the issue is really about

- Be patient

- Agree to disagree

- Be respectful

Listen and Understand

My uncle, Karl "Yock" Flemke, former president of Junior Achievement, taught me at an early age how to truly listen to another without distraction. He had the uncanny ability to make you feel like the only person who mattered when he listened to a story. Listening is the key to effective communication. It can be easy to get distracted by texts, calls, or other interruptions or jump into problem-solving mode before hearing someone out. Give people your undivided attention and the space they need to talk, and actively listen to them. This means listen to hear. A lot of times "the issue" is not the issue at all; make it your goal to understand beyond the words.

Be Patient

Throughout the communication process, have your patience shoes on. The conversation could be slow. You might need to give people time to cool down, collect their thoughts, or figure out what's truly on their mind. And you might need to do the same in order to respond appropriately.

Agree to Disagree

Be okay with not seeing eye to eye. Having faith is not about making the other person move to your side. It is about being respectful while having a productive dialogue. Be willing to listen, share, and discuss. Be willing to disagree while maintaining respect in the conversation and for each other. And be open to the creativity that can arise from differing opinions.

Be Respectful

Cut people some slack. Uncertainty and change bring stress along with them, and there are as many ways to respond to stress as there are people. Leaders can bring assurance and calm by modeling respect for individual points of view and concerns while firmly creating an environment of safety and trust.

Time to revisit the story of Mr. Jones. When he came to me upset about his salesperson taking the call while walking the dog, I took time to listen. I held the space for him to express his thoughts and concerns. But then the real work started as I explored the "why" behind Mr. Jones's reaction. It turns out he was triggered by this small event that represented a major change. Unlike his employee, he was never able to walk his dog while working. He was both jealous and confused over the social norms of working from home.

After getting to the bottom of Mr. Jones's reaction, together, we were able to talk about how he was managing the transition to working from home with his employees. We talked in a calm manner about how he agrees and disagrees with what the salesperson did. As a result of our discussion, Mr. Jones felt heard and supported and was able to move past his anger into understanding. More importantly, he set up guidelines for how to work in this new hybrid world for his employees and his customers.

BUILD TRUST

Trust is a two-way street. Many business leaders come from a traditional mindset that trust needs to be earned, and this serves as the foundation for their workplace culture. As a result, these leaders treat employees as if they have something to prove. When you do not empower employees to make even the smallest decisions, for example, you're saying you do not trust them. Believe me, your employees know this and feel it. If an employee does not feel like their leader trusts them, how can you build mutual faith and trust?

I had a prospective client tell me before the pandemic of 2020 that they would not consider allowing remote work because they did not trust their employees to actually do the work. This is an old, outdated model of thought, long gone in well-functioning organizations today, just like faxing and phone conference calling. Helping employees navigate change from a place of respect creates trust and is a great first step in our new way of working.

An employee who feels trusted also feels valued. As a result, workplace satisfaction and productivity increase with employees reporting they believe their work is more worthwhile.[3] As the lines between home life and work life blur in our work-from-home society, the need for trust increases. One method of instilling trust is first creating an environment of faith. If your

---

3   Julian Birkinshaw, Jordan Cohen, and Pawel Stach, "Research: Knowledge Workers Are More Productive from Home," *Harvard Business Review*, August 31, 2020, https://hbr.org/2020/08/research-knowledge-workers-are-more-productive-from-home/.

employees feel safe taking an active role in helping the company and clients get through change, you're on the right track. Trust is seen in words and actions. Provide both to your employees.

BREAK THE MOLD

We are all navigating this new workplace together. It is like being a toddler and having a world around you that is scary but full of exciting new opportunities. We are breaking the status quo for not only how we work together but for what work looks like for future generations.

> We are breaking the status quo for not only how we work together but for what work looks like for future generations.

"The sum of us is stronger than any one of us" may sound cliché, but it's true and important to keep in mind. All levels of employees in your workplace need to deeply understand that we need to lead together. We have survived this crisis and will survive others, big and small, together. There are no guidelines for moving forward in this new way of working. But that is great for you and your employees. We are all pioneers.

If you're doing things the way other companies

are doing them, stop. Do it your way. Make the new model fit your company culture. There are all kinds of tools, new and old, that help you and your employees create something special and unique to your company culture. For example, redesign your workspace to create physical space for your employees, customers, and other visitors to feel safe; create a schedule of staggered workdays; alternate months that people can choose to work in the office or out of the office; create cross-departmental teams that work on certain days of the week.

Employees want to work for a company that matches their values and isn't simply a place they work. Be curious and explore your company's core values together. Discuss them with your employees and make them more than just words. Live and breathe what makes your company culture unique. That is what gets people excited to go to work and become genuine ambassadors for your brand.

MAKE IT FUN

Want to attract and retain top talent? Want to have your employees show up to work engaged and invested in the outcome of their day? Then make your workplace fun. Treat your employees like they are human beings, not just a name on your payroll.

Every week, I meet with my key leaders to keep our connection, communication, and planning processes going strong. Every month, I meet with the whole team in a hybrid setting. We have people on the screen and people in the room. To create a fun and inclusive experience, we send lunch to the people who are remote. If we are breaking for lunch, we have the remote people go out for a special lunch and expense it. It is never going to be all of the experience. It's going to be a different experience. We all have to be a part of this new process and have faith that we will each fully participate and contribute to the team effort.

We all have to be a part of this new process and have faith that we will each fully participate and contribute to the team effort.

Get creative. Go on scavenger hunts, meet for a happy hour, arrange a group escape room, or have a fireside chat. You can do these activities live, virtually, or in hybrid mode. Go on a virtual walk or take a walking meeting. But don't leave your people to hang out without you all the time. The most important thing is being present with them. Create fun in the workplace and encourage connections with your employees. Build the groundwork for faith through trust, transparency, and communication.

When your back's against the wall
Just turn around and see
I'll be there, I'll catch your fall
So have a little faith in me.

—JOHN HIATT

Faith in Practice

What you can do to build faith:

- People are unsettled and afraid of all the changes hitting them at once. Help them build faith in one another and in you by communicating effectively, building trust, breaking the mold of tradition, and making it fun to work together.

- Build trust by reacting from a place of positive intent to overcome the challenges of negativity and high emotion.

- Circle back to the notion and practice of leading together. This will make you all stronger and more aligned.

- Begin communicating by listening first.

- Trust that employees will get the work done from wherever they are working.

- Use the opportunity change offers to create your own unique work culture, not a copy of what others are doing.

Reflection & Notes

As a leader and pioneer in this challenging time, what will you let go of in order to create space for the new?

CHAPTER 2

THE EMPLOYEE EXPERIENCE

No one cares how much you know, until they know how much you care.

—THEODORE ROOSEVELT

"Neal," the husband of one of my longtime remote employees, "Josie," has been working from home during the pandemic. They also have two young children who have been learning online from home. This is the first time the entire family has been together every hour, every day, over a long period of time—and they *love it! They have lunch together, take breaks outside together, and have more time for love and fun throughout the day with flexibility to get the work done at whatever time of day works. Plus, Neal has been saving ninety minutes in commute time each day and has devoted those hours to his work. As a result, he has been more productive overall working from home over the past year. Now that things are opening up, and for no other reason than it's "normal" for everyone to work at the same place, Neal's employer has indicated that he will have no choice but to go back to the office full time. Neal, Josie, and the children all want him to continue working at home, but Neal's employer insists on everyone being back at the office full time. This scenario is happening in at least 30 percent of companies across the country.*

Many families have become used to living a new kind of life, one that makes them more connected. We are rebuilding American families, just as we are reimagining our workplaces. They are no longer separate entities but a holistic blend of work and home lives. Leaders must recognize and embrace these new realities because their employees already have. It is no longer acceptable to mandate employees to return to the office. That opens the door to losing critical talent. The best leaders know that they must invite or request people to work on-site again. They must throw away "command and control" to offer individuals choices and flexibility and, at the same time, build equality and inclusiveness into their cultures.

PUT PEOPLE FIRST

In the best of times, great leaders put their people first. In a crisis like the pandemic, people-centered leadership is essential, making it more natural to feel empathy, passion, and concern for the well-being of people first, before anything else. In the absence of trusting relationships, employees cannot perform. With them, they are fully capable of moving us out of any crisis.

People-centered leaders share a number of important attributes that support productive relationships and healthy cultures as well as business success. They connect deeply with their people by telling the truth, showing competence and accountability, building trust through empowerment, listening well, and encouraging innovation. These are the things that create a positive and inspiring employee experience that helps attract and retain the people you want in your company.

Our past focus on the notions of "employee journeys" and "moments that matter" seems simplistic as we move on to resolve growing and more pressing employee concerns about health, safety, transportation, tools for working productively from home, personal finances, team communications, fatigue, general feeling of being overwhelmed, *and* desire for more time with family.

THE CULTURE SHIFT

There was a culture shift in 2020 when the concept of employee engagement was replaced by "employee experience." This new perspective on how employees should be treated in the workplace requires us, as employers, to create the same positive experience inside our companies that we provide at the customer level.

Think about walking into Nordstrom versus Target or the Ritz versus Motel Eight. They are typically very different experiences. At the Ritz, everything is "my pleasure," and at many a Motel Eight, you're lucky if they look at you. Although upscale does not always mean better service, it is often the case that high-end customers expect and get better service.

Every customer experience is unique to a company, and the same is true for the employee experience.

Think about it this way. Employees are your internal customers. If the employee experience is great, guess who else has a great experience? The customer. But how do you get there? How do you create that unique experi-

> **Employee experience is about mutually beneficial relationships between leadership and employees.**

ence? Employee experience is about mutually beneficial relationships between leadership and employees.

Leaders can develop better relationships by:

- Creating shared goals together

- Showing people their thoughts and contributions are valued

- Reconnecting personally with people as they return to work

- Understanding employees' individual strengths and interests

- Committing to share more information about performance and results

CAMELOT COMMUNITIES

Employee experience is an ongoing process. Bringing love, well-being, inclusivity, and shared purpose into the workplace takes all-hands-on-deck effort. Creating a healthy and happy organization takes constant work, like a garden. You cannot plant the seeds and not water them. Seeds grow into gardens only when they are nurtured.

> You cannot plant the seeds and not water them. Seeds grow into gardens only when they are nurtured.

Camelot communities bloom into communities in positive environments where people find dignity in the work they do. Work is no longer work—it is a calling, and people are fully engaged, driven, and passionate about what they do. The work is just as meaningful as the relationships people develop with leadership and coworkers.

I've hit that Camelot Community twice in my life as an employer. In both situations, coming to work felt like joining a community. We loved being with one another, taking time to genuinely care, joke, break bread, drink, laugh, and cry together. The first time was in Boston, many years ago, with my team of Scott Ragusa and Michelle Desaulniers. We were unstoppable! We celebrated our wins, analyzed our failures, and rose again to win, together. My most recent Camelot Community was gifted to me by my current staff with a love letter in June 2020.

It is impossible to recreate perfection, so do not even try, and you certainly cannot force it into being. However, we can all aspire to it and do all that we can to create those memorable moments that form a Camelot Community, which is as close to perfection as we can get. Actively listen to your employees on all levels. Check in with them daily, weekly, monthly, and annually. Use the feedback you get to make meaningful changes. Let your people know you listened, heard, and reacted to their feedback.

SHOW ME THE RECOGNITION

Taking care of people and supporting their journey is an employer's job. We work for our employees just as much as they work for us. It is a difficult and complex process to build better humans, including ourselves. Make sure people know they matter and show that their thoughts, opinions, and contributions are valued. The number one reason people leave companies is because they do not feel like they are appreciated. If people do not get recognition from you, they will leave and find it elsewhere.

Recognition can range from simple and low cost to extravagant, depending on the reason for it and your budget. Pair recognition with something tangible. Words are great, but they do not last and can quickly be forgotten. An example of pairing words with a tangible form of recognition comes from a California client of mine. On payday, he has the hourly workers come into the office for a catered lunch. Before they leave, he hands each of them their paycheck and personally thanks them. In addition, each employee brings a friend or two who would be a great fit to join their community! It is brilliant: recognition, appreciation, and recruitment all in one!

> **If people do not get recognition from you, they will leave and find it elsewhere.**

Beyond the workplace, moments matter too. Our personal and professional lives are blended holistically within each of us, and we experience our "whole selves" even more in today's blended work settings, which may be on-site, at home, or a hybrid. Distance makes it more important that you take time to celebrate special moments with your employees, from births to marriages and other occasions important to your employees. Connect fiercely with your people wherever they are located and however you can express how much you appreciate them.

What if you believe you already have a strong recognition program but it's not working? The answer is, you're doing it wrong! Think about your customers for a minute. You make certain you know how they want to be served and what they want—and you provide it. The same is true for your employees. Take time to understand their needs and preferences; respect their individuality (e.g., introvert or extrovert); and find appropriate and meaningful ways to recognize them.

Ideas for how to recognize introverts:

- Note mailed to their home

- Book

- Gift certificate for coffee

- Certificate of appreciation/plaque/framed item awarded privately or in a small group

Ideas for how to recognize extroverts:

- Certificate of appreciation/plaque/framed item presented at a small or large event

- Verbal appreciation in front of a group

- Tickets to events (sports/opera/etc.)

Ideas for how to celebrate families:

- Tickets to a baseball game or movie theater

- Gift certificate for ice cream

Ideas for recognizing stretch goals/above-and-beyond achievements:

- Airline tickets

- Hotel/destination gift certificate

> **The secret weapon to connection is authenticity. Be genuine with recognition. Be thoughtful. Show your people you pay attention.**

The secret weapon to connection is authenticity. Be genuine with recognition. Be thoughtful. Show your people you pay attention. Know your audience and give them what's most meaningful to them.

TRUST DOES NOT JUST HAPPEN

During the pandemic, a member of my team told me she realized she trusted everything I was saying even in the middle of this crisis. She trusted because I had always told her the truth. She found relief and a little peace in knowing that she could at least count on one thing during the upheaval all around her; she could trust that everything I said about our company and her work was the truth. No need to question or worry about anything.

Lying is never okay whether you're a leader or an employee. That includes leaving something out in place of lying, which isn't being truthful either. The key to trust is transparency. You achieve transparency by selecting the right people who fit into a culture built on being fair, reasonable, and accountable to your shared values and practices.

Transparency cannot be some of the time. It has to be all of the time. The more transparent you are, the more

> **Transparency cannot be some of the time. It has to be all of the time.**

people will believe in you and what you say. Share openly what good behavior looks like within your company and model that for your employees. Do this and they will trust you all of the time.

It is not simply about what we create for our employees. It's about what they create for themselves and each other. We are intertwined naturally and in various ways at work. But trust has to be built. Trust does not just happen because you wake up on a Monday and say, "I am going to make sure we get in a little trust today." Trust happens when you are consistent, repetitive, and disciplined about transparency and honesty. People easily sniff it out when you're being disingenuous.

ADVENTURE INTO TRANSPARENCY

We have been taught by our parents, teachers, and employers to leave our personal lives at home. Leaders have to pave the way and guide employees to teach, model, and support transparency. Being transparent isn't easy for many of us. Our models, whether parents, teachers, or employers, have often left out details and told half-truths to protect or aggrandize themselves. As leaders of our companies, we can model something different through a willingness to be both vulnerable and transparent.

What we get by being truthful is trusting, respectful relationships and high levels of productivity. Be consistent and practice transparency regularly. Probe with care and empathy. Employees may not trust enough to believe you the first time you engage. Your willingness to share is essential in breaking through stereotypes of traditional employee/employer relationships and building trusting ones.

The first step in encouraging transparency is

modeling it and sharing yourself. Your people want to know you are human. When I start a workshop, I begin by sharing my story. Part of my history is that I am a cancer survivor. At one point, all within a sixty-day time frame, I had a baby and was diagnosed with cancer. Two years later, I was let go from my job. In sharing my history, pain about my journey, family, and personal struggles, I connect deeply with my audience and my employees based on real emotions.

The second step in becoming transparent is having open conversations with your employees to gain understanding of new people and check in with those who've been with you over the long term. People choose to work with people, not companies.

Some key questions I ask to gain insight are:

- Is there anything in your life that might affect your ability to be 100 percent on the journey with us?

- Why do you choose to work for me?

- Under what circumstances would you leave?

- How can we best support you in doing your work?

- How do you best respond to feedback?

Invite your employees to share and let go of any fear of judgment. Being asked to leave our personal lives at the door has never really been possible, but employers and employees both pretended that it was. Today, in our work-from-home environment, we understand that we are whole people and cannot separate ourselves into parts. And as a result of the pandemic, companies will forever *be* in their employees' homes and lives on a daily basis.

HOP OFF THE FENCE

No one can be led by a wishy-washy leader. Lead with empathy, understanding, and no judgment, but be decisive. Develop and convey clear guidelines for how to participate in work, what to expect of each role, and how to communicate.

There are many different opinions and options for in-person, virtual, and remote work. People get to choose how they participate in meetings or work, and everyone on the team has to respect the choices their coworkers make. It is leaders' responsibility to make each session, whether in person, remote, or hybrid, inclusive and each audience as important as the other.

Be decisive in communicating what you need from employees and showing that you recognize their needs as well. There are no sides of the fence to be on here. All of us will need to figure out the best ways to work together. Helping your employees be comfortable with sharing and participating takes thought and effort and will result in better relationships and greater productivity.

Now, more than ever, people have fears about what they say, how they say it, and who they say it to. Many people feel censored and shamed for sharing what's in their heart. This judgment usually stems from fear. When people are scared, they lash out at others. Have candid conversations with your people. Take the time to understand and appreciate their thoughts, fears, and needs even if you do not feel the same way. Empathy is one of the most important qualities leaders can show employees.

SHUT UP AND LISTEN

Start to build trust by giving it. We hire people to do a job. Micromanaging creates frustration and low job satisfaction. Let employees do their job by creating a safety net, respecting their skills, and trusting them to do the work. The safety net is setting performance expectations and inspecting the end product. Trust your employees to get the job done, and they will feel valued, respected, and find meaning in their work. These are major keys to retention.

When your team comes to you with ideas and feedback, look at them and listen. We are all talking too much. Renowned researcher Albert Mehrabian found that 90 percent of communication comes from and is interpreted by nonverbal behaviors.[4] Listen actively with your body language. Allow employees to take chances and trust them to do their work. Allowing risk-taking and encouraging innovation on your team feed creative juices. When you make the journey fun, employees become invested in the outcomes of their work. It is the journey that matters.

FIT TO QUIT

The reality is that some people are with you just for this moment in their journey. They check in for a year or two, six months, three years, five years, and then they are onto the next thing. Why should that be bad? Wouldn't you rather have an incredible employee for the brief period of their journey they want to be with you contributing whatever they have to offer?

---

4   Jeff Thompson, "Is Nonverbal Communication a Numbers Game?" *Psychology Today*, September 30, 2011, https:// www.psychologytoday.com/us/blog/beyond-words/201109/ is-nonverbal-communication-numbers-game.

From an employer perspective, we believe that if someone quits us, it is a bad thing. We have been taught that high turnover is bad. And certainly, if you do not manage turnover, you have got a larger issue at hand. Part of good leadership, though, is helping people exit when you need someone in the role but know this particular individual is not a fit. Part of creating a healthy employee experience is making sure that the people working for you want to be with you and cycling people in and out as things change. If they do not

> **Part of good leadership is helping people exit when you need someone in the role but know this particular individual is not a fit.**

fit you, they are going to quit you. If they do not fit you, invite them to leave before productivity or morale is damaged.

Letting an employee go opens up room for that next incredible person to join your team. It does not mean these people were bad. It means they did not fit you. Have grace with employees when they are ready to move on to their next journey. Foster an environment of trust, support, and respect for the dignity of the individual and the protection of your reputation and values.

PEAKS AND VALLEYS

Companies do not grow in straight lines. Communities do not grow in straight lines. Relationships do not grow in straight lines. We have peaks and valleys in the customer experience and the employee experience. It is the trend line that matters, not the moment in time. Be aware of the trends, measure them to manage them. Concentrate your day-to-day efforts on building an employee experience that attracts and retains the talent you need to deliver on your goals.

On the other hand, we expect our efforts will lead to constant growth and we become frustrated with setbacks. Pushing through the valleys is hard and elusive. Success takes time, effort, energy, love, patience, and kindness. You have to be okay with the tough but real emotions of irritation and disappointment you feel when your company isn't growing as fast as you planned. Instead, remember that you're fostering a community that serves other people and your business.

Building Your Camelot

Sharpen Your Engagement Skills

Practice people-centered leadership, showing empathy, passion, and concern for the well-being of your people first, before anything else. Know that you hire a human with all their complexities and relationships.

- Explain your WHYs; people want to know.

- Listen to employees when defining return-to-work plans.

- Do not mandate that people return to work on-site; invite or request instead, and let individuals choose what works best for them.

- Have the courage to be authentic, vulnerable, and consistently transparent.

- Recognize and reward people in the way they personally prefer to be celebrated.

- Understand that as a leader it is okay not to know.

- Be aware of trends, and spend time building your Camelot Community.

Reflection & Notes

In reimagining your workplace as a Camelot Community, what things do you want to keep about your culture and what things need to go?

CHAPTER 3

LEADING WITH EMPATHY

*Empathy is ... communicating that incredibly
healing message of "You're not alone."*

—BRENÉ BROWN, PHD, LMSW

Most people do not know how to truly understand someone else's point of view without letting their thoughts, opinions, and emotions get in the way. We sit in our own place of judgment rather than using empathy as the bridge to understanding and connection.

EMPATHY—FORGET ABOUT YOU

Empathy is about taking time to listen, putting yourself in someone else's place, and sharing feelings.

> **Empathy is about taking time to listen, putting yourself in someone else's place, and sharing feelings.**

It is not about sugarcoating, jumping into problem-solving, or having to agree. It is meeting people where they are now, listening, and providing what they need in that moment. Do not make your opinions and feelings center stage. Showing empathy is about them, not you.

One of the wonderful people who has helped me build my company taught me to "seek to understand" first. By observing her empathy with our team, I learned more with each interaction. Every issue you face with your company or employees is an opportunity to seek understanding, learn, and grow. That is the value of empathy every leader needs to understand.

If we want to connect with people on deeper levels, and I hope we do, we need to shift from a total focus on *what* people do into *why* they do it. Communication guru Simon Sinek always says to focus on the human connection. When I am speaking at live events, I'll start with feelings and embracing emotion as a way to connect with my audience. The same basic concept applies to leaders interacting with their people: embrace the emotion of the moment.

Author Marcus Buckingham said two questions every leader should ask their people are: What are you working on? How can I help you? These two questions are simple but powerful—they let your employees share their top priorities, show you trust them to do their jobs, and let you fulfill your role as a leader in supporting them. Ask the questions, be quiet, and let your people talk.

> **Ask the questions, be quiet, and let your people talk.**

INVISIBLE VULNERABILITIES

We all have invisible vulnerabilities: small, medium, and big. And we all have had life experiences, good and bad, that cannot be seen with the eyes. You do not know what anyone else has experienced, and they don't know what you have been through. For example, you did not know I had cancer until I told you in the last chapter. You do not know that four years ago I lost my dad, which left a large hole in my heart.

I am not making it about me. Sharing is not making it about yourself. It is about opening up on a more personal level and having the courage to be vulnerable. Leaders often do not think about showing vulnerability to their employees, but when you do, you are entering a more meaningful relationship that is personal for both of you—making both leader and employee more human.

Our shared humanity makes for happier, more productive workplaces. We all have our own personal journeys that shaped our lives and continue to shape them. Respect those journeys, yours and theirs. You cannot see, touch, or feel what another person is going through unless you are willing to hold space for them. Be a willing listener, and be aware that sometimes you have to be the first to share, giving way to mutual sharing.

SHAKESPEARIAN PLAY OF LIFE

Like actors in a Shakespearian play, we play roles versus showing up authentically. We have been taught to hide our true selves, show up a certain way, and display a false sense of bravado in front of others. What mask are you wearing today? Do you wear different ones at

> **Like actors in a Shakespearian play, we play roles versus showing up authentically.**

work, home, and with friends?

I can walk into a room where I've been invited to speak and see people sitting there with their arms tightly crossed over their chest. They are beginning to doubt before I even open my mouth. What do you have to say? What are you going to do? What are you bringing me of value today? Even as strangers about to spend an hour or so together, our tendency to judge is apparent. That tendency only increases as we move to online interactions.

The posture we take in approaching others, including both employees and employer, can either shut people down or engage them. Even more than when a speaker faces her audience, in our work-from-home video environments, we are seeing nonverbal body language up close. There have been many studies about nonverbals; they comprise 50 to 85 percent of the communication experience—and the same holds true whether you're interacting in person or online.[5] When you're on video, make sure you do not have a "resting Zoom face" that might be misinterpreted. All of the faces, torsos, and eyes of meeting attendees are focused and in front of you

---

5   The University of Texas Permian Basin, "How Much of Communication Is Nonverbal?" accessed May 2021, https://online.utpb.edu/about-us/articles/communication/how-much-of-communication-is-nonverbal/.

simultaneously like Hollywood stars.

However you're interacting, start with a smile. Look with genuine interest while you engage in small talk. The whole person matters. What is going on in their life beyond the face on the screen matters. As you communicate, try to understand their point of view and their emotions, both positive and negative. A smile, your full attention, and kind eyes say that you care and are ready to support them.

You will have people on your team who have a jaded view of life, difficulty trusting, or a fear of being vulnerable. And maybe this is you. To lead with empathy, get beyond the first layer of nicety, the facade we all walk around with. Lead with your willingness to dig deep, listen, and model mutual support.

Being empathic is learning how to be your authentic self. If you show up with defenses and blind spots, you're not going to be open or aware, have empathy for others, or create meaningful relationships with your employees. A leader's job isn't just to manage their talent. You're there to help people along in their journey, make good decisions, and ensure working for you is part of a great life. How you lead isn't just about your people; what you invest in your employees will come back to you and your business manyfold.

BREAKOUT FOR THE LADIES

Recently I was in a meeting with other CEOs, all male except for me. The question before us was whether people will return to the office postpandemic. All of the male CEOs agreed that yes, they would come back. I, the lone woman, said "No, they are not coming back." This experience made me realize that I need to take a moment here to address women, although I hope this section will interest everyone and help you better connect with and understand the experiences of women in your company.

The fact is COVID-19 has had an outsized impact on gender equality. Although both men and women have been negatively impacted, women have been hit much harder. According to research by Accenture, women have less work, less income, and less job security now than before the pandemic, and the gender gap has widened, extending the estimated time to gender equality by fifty-one years.[6] Society, including business, has largely been made by men for men. It is women who will remain at home taking care of children and homeschooling until daycares reopen and it is safe for kids to return to school.

---

6   Accenture, "Working to accelerate equality for all," accessed
     May 2021, https://www.accenture.com/hk-en/about/
     inclusion-diversity/gender-equality.

If you're like many women, when you *are* able to be at work, you may be hiding your true self. We are often afraid to show up as the strong, feminine beings we are. Instead, we dress like men or become homogenous. The way women act in the workplace can hold different labels than if men displayed those same qualities and behaviors. I've been called a "witch" so many times in my life because I am direct and like to tell it like it is—qualities men are typically lauded for.

If you display an emotional or vulnerable side, it is seen as normal, but it also carries the risk of being seen as flighty or weak. As an emotionally open woman, you may find that others assume you cannot be both vulnerable and strong, and you might be passed over for certain roles as a result. There's a good chance you have already experienced this, and maybe more than once.

Years of research by organizations like the nonprofit Catalyst show that greater gender equality benefits all of society: men and women, rich and poor, young and old. Not just the right thing to do, gender equality brings more inclusive and accurate decision-making; more innovation resulting in growth; better health; increased education; greater economic stability; and stronger workplace cultures. Additionally, expectations for equality are only going to increase as younger generations, who are more concerned with culture, continue to join the workforce.

Although there has been progress here and there, the decades-old statistics related to gaps in pay and opportunity still reflect women's reality in 2021. It is not just wages that are lopsided for women. Although women-owned businesses continue to grow at a fast pace in our country, they lag behind businesses run by their male counterparts in funding, number of employees, and revenue. This, despite the fact that companies with the most women on their executive teams outperform companies with the fewest women. You'd be wrong to assume that companies seek out skilled leaders who could increase performance—at least if they are women. Instead, women are more likely to be promoted to leadership positions during times of crisis or economic downturn where there's a higher risk of failure, in what's often known as "falling off the glass cliff."

Most adults believe that male and female leaders have different leadership styles, but few think one gender's approach is better overall, according to Pew Research.[7] However, while men are seen as more willing to take risks, women leaders are perceived to

---

7   Pew Research Center, "Women and Leadership," January 14, 2015, https://www.pewresearch.org/social-trends/2015/01/14/women-and-leadership/.

be stronger in traits like compassion, compromise, and to our point in this chapter, empathy. These traits make women highly suitable to lead in the most challenging situations.

> **It is time we make empathy and other "feminine" traits that help ensure great leadership the norm.**

It is time we make empathy and other "feminine" traits that help ensure great leadership the norm. Most women are great at daring to care; now more of us need to dare to stand up strongly for ourselves so we can contribute fully to our communities.

NICE TOUCHES

Communication and connection can be accomplished in a variety of modes: verbal; nonverbal; spoken in person or by phone; and written in texts, emails, and handwritten notes. I affectionately call these "touches." The more personal they are, the more appreciated they are by individual employees. And the more frequent they are, the more they build morale and increase retention.

Leaders set the foundation for communication in their organizations. Do it based on understanding and respecting how your people want to be touched. Give people options to choose how to show up in the way they feel most comfortable. Define what good communication looks like for your company, beginning with clear expectations for how you measure productivity and performance for each role.

MAKE SPACE FOR CONNECTION

In the work-from-home, work-from-anywhere environment, it is difficult to get personal and make meaningful connections. As we are all experiencing, it is easier to build a community when we are physically together. We now have the barrier of the screen, and like it or not, we have to embrace the medium we are in right now.

Some people are reluctant to connect through video: they do not want to be seen, do not like how they look on camera, may not be comfortable sharing what their home workspace looks like, and other excuses. Yes, video makes us more vulnerable; and, yes, it will continue to be an important way to keep our connections going.

As a whole, employees are missing connection in this moment. Extroverts want to be with others; they thrive on touch and direct social stimulation.

Introverts are struggling because they like to occasionally hang out with the extroverts around the watercooler, in the break room, or in meetings to enjoy their energy and join in the conversation

At the same time, leaders need to respect how exhausting virtual and video meetings can be. Give yourself and employees permission to be natural and not stare with laser eyes into their cameras. Keep meetings under an hour to increase attention and prevent mental fatigue.

Make time for more social and genuine connections in virtual meetings. Open meetings with time for small talk that would happen in office settings. Create breakout rooms during meetings to keep employees engaged. Have fun with virtual coffee chats, scavenger hunts, trivia nights, or happy hours. Take time to personally connect with your employees at least once or twice a week outside of meetings.

GIVE THEM WHAT THEY NEED

There's a growing economic inequality crisis with remote workers not having money for or access to technology. Gallup's Employee Engagement Survey revealed workers fear not having what they need to do their job.[8] The old paradigm would be to let those employees go and not provide support. Choose empathy instead.

No one wants to lose out on high-quality talent because they live in an area where it is hard to get affordable high-speed internet or they lack the funds to

> **There's a growing economic inequality crisis with remote workers not having money for or access to technology.**

have a dedicated work computer. Create a program to provide laptops, internet, phones, or other office equipment and technology for your employees so they can have a functional setup in their personal space. And there's more you can provide in terms of support.

Sometimes the internet goes down, and sometimes your employee might need a change of scenery, if the kids are at home for example. Look into alternative work environments. Companies like Office Evolution have private, shared, and coworking spaces across the United States. Secure one or more rooms in these spaces for your employees and make them available to book. Not only will your employees have an emergency location for internet or power issues but they may have the opportunity to connect with

---

8   Gallup, "The Power of Gallup's Q12 Employee Engage-
     ment Survey," accessed May 2021, https://www.gallup.com/
     access/323333/q12-employee-engagement-survey.aspx.

coworkers in a live setting. Invest in your employees and they will invest in you.

BOUNDARIES ARE BEAUTIFUL

Working in a remote or hybrid setting has thrown off a lot of employees. They do not have the luxury of separating work and home life in the same way they used to. It was easy to have barriers and work/life balance when we commuted to the office.

While some people might have a home office, many are working from their dining-room table, living-room couch, bedroom, or countertop. Their workspace looks at them all the time. Helping employees create a space where they can turn work on and off boosts productivity, enhances connection, and creates a healthier work/life balance. Both employer and employee need to respect the boundaries of work and personal life. Setting virtual-world boundaries also includes clear and helpful guidelines on how to interact at work. Foster an environment of respect that would take place in traditional work meetings: only one person talks at a time, no side chatter, and other agreed-upon rules of engagement.

EMBRACE LEADING WITH EMPATHY

Do you know your people well enough to lead them in the most effective way? Do you build empathic relationships with them? Are you empathic enough that if someone behaves differently than they normally do, you'd pause, observe, and ask how you can be helpful?

Having a candid conversation with an employee about noticing them behave differently than usual shouldn't come from a place of judgment. You're observing and opening the door for conversation. Leading with empathy means understanding and accepting that people are not always operating at their very best. Issues from home affect work lives, and issues at work affect personal lives. Working within and around that reality is the best way to create a place where people want to come to work.

Leading with empathy is about holding up the mirror for others to see themselves in a mindset of growth and support. As a leader, if you care about where your employees are going on their journey, you will want to be the mirror for them and have your employees do the same for you.

Empathy is about listening and taking in other people's points of view, having the courage to lead with vulnerability, and making collaborative decisions you believe are best for the organization. Some decisions might be unpopular. Disagreement does not mean disrespect. Leading with empathy means leading with transparency, fairness, and respect—ensuring that all points of view are heard.

> **Disagreement does not mean disrespect.**

YOU NEVER WALK ALONE

The good news is we are all going through this together. The bad news is we are all going through this together. Change is happening right now, everywhere, and we are struggling. No one really knows the best solutions, and there isn't a single solution that fits all companies.

Change, whether good or bad, is never easy. What will help is leaders taking the initiative to communicate with their people at a more regular and frequent cadence to champion change. Leaders do not have all the answers. Make that okay for yourself. Get all of your team members involved in learning, testing, and trying out ideas. Make them feel heard and supported. Be gentle with yourself and have empathy for your people.

Flex Your Empathy Muscles

- Seek to understand, not judge.

- Listen first; stand in the shoes of others; share who you are.

- Create meaningful relationships with a willingness to be vulnerable.

- See your people holistically; they have personal lives that come to work with them.

- Communicate with employees transparently, authentically, and frequently.

- Provide remote workers with whatever flexibility and technical support they need to succeed.

- Make time for genuine and social connections—and fun—in virtual meetings.

- Set boundaries for interaction and work/life balance.

Reflection & Notes

How comfortable are you being a vulnerable leader? What are your fears, if any? How do you think your vulnerability facilitates becoming a more empathic leader and in what ways do you think empathy will benefit your work relationships?

CHAPTER 4

BUILDING COMMUNITY

Shower the people you love with love. Show them the way you feel. Things are gonna be much better if you only will.

—JAMES TAYLOR

You're not building a company; you're building a community that is about relationship, trust, and common values. Everyone in your community is centered around a single purpose—to serve common clients. Just as every company is unique, so are the communities they develop.

Communities are all around us. They are not just

found in churches, neighborhoods, or businesses. When you belong to a local sports club, an Elks or Rotary Club, or a hunting or hobby group, you are in a community. Even the groups of friends you golf or enjoy other activities with are forms of community. We can have a

> You're not building a company; you're building a community that is about relationship, trust, and common values.

community with a handful of people or thousands, tied together by shared interests or experience. Most communities have leaders, and it is their responsibility to make sure communities work for members. Although all communities change over time, today workplace communities are off the charts with change.

Workspace is radically different now than it was prepandemic. Technology and work from home have redesigned our idea of what an office is. Remote and hybrid employees bring their coworkers into their homes, and now homes, along with families and pets, are part of the work community. Navigating this shift can be overwhelming for everyone. At this moment, people are scared. They want to be listened to; they want to be treated as the individuals they are, and they want to be safe. They want to feel like they are their company's most valuable asset, which they are.

CULTURE RETREAT

In the midst of this dramatic change, we have fallen into a sort of culture retreat where many leaders are confused. They do not know how to build community or if they should even be focused on company culture in this moment. *Culture* is an old word for community. We use words like *culture* and *engagement*, but does anyone really know what those words mean or how to measure them?

Think about engagement on social media, as an example. What does that entail? It looks different on each platform and changes value, from the number of likes one month to being all about shares the next. There is no commonality for participants. It is time to do away with the terms *culture* and *engagement* and shift to the concepts of community and employee experience. Everyone knows what a community means and what experiencing it feels like.

We have talked about the customer experience for years, and an excellent experience means catering to individual customer needs. Now, we need to do the same for our employees who are experiencing their companies in different ways: some on-site, some at home, some in various hybrid situations. It is up to leaders to create community out of these various employee experiences—and their struggles provide an opportunity for HR to step forward and be the hero. HR understands how to build listening, fairness, inclusiveness, flexibility, and celebration into community and has the tech tools to make it happen in diverse ways. They can be a leader's greatest resource. Rely on them for ideas and support.

POSTTRAUMATIC JOB SYNDROME

The old model of running a company, top-down management and little flexibility or humanity, has created unprecedented stress, fear, and lack of trust in the modern workplace. A HuffPost article has coined this concept as Posttraumatic Job Disorder.[9] I know people who are scared to start new jobs.

Comments I frequently hear include:

- Oh, we'll see if they actually are what they say they are.

- I do not trust what they say.

- My previous employer pulled all kinds of things and played games.

---

9   Rena DeLevie, "Post-Traumatic Job Disorder," Huffpost.
    com, February 24, 2015, https://www.huffpost.com/entry/
    post-traumatic-job-disord_b_6740326.

- My paychecks have bounced before.

- They changed my schedule without asking me.

- They created a toxic work environment.

- They pit people against each other.

- They would pick favorites, making it impossible to get promotions.

- I saw hardworking people let go without warning.

- I do not feel safe saying anything.

The concept of work-related PTSD has been studied by occupational psychologists across various work environments. People in high-stress jobs who are exposed to trauma, such as medical workers, police officers, and firefighters are often the only groups we associate with workplace PTSD. However, anyone from a bank teller to a sales representative can be at risk for developing PTSD from their work experiences. The good news is that work-related PTSD can decrease over time with exposure to positive environments that rebuild trust or a sense of safety at work.[10]

---

10   M. Skogstad, M. Skorstad, A. Lie, H. S. Conradi, T. Heir,
      L. Weisæth, "Work-related post-traumatic stress disorder,"
      Occupational Medicine 3, no. 63, April 2013: 175–182,
      https://doi.org/10.1093/occmed/kqt003.

But why does this happen in the first place? Leaders who do not communicate openly, clearly, and regularly about what they expect and why need to step right out of that selfish mindset where everything is about the company's or owner's wants, needs, or pocketbook. They might have gotten away with that in the past, but thankfully, that form of leadership is no longer acceptable.

> **Today, if you want to attract and retain top talent, you must treat your employees with respect and empathy and communicate way more than you think is necessary.**

Today, if you want to attract and retain top talent, you must treat your employees with respect and empathy and communicate way more than you think is necessary. Equally important, you need to reward and celebrate employee achievements as part of your communication and performance programs. Lack of recognition is the number one reason people quit—and recognizing people is such an easy, fun thing to do!

Remember Camelot? In our new reality, there are so many ways to build community, whether you're together in an office, virtually, or a hybrid. People have their own comfort level about coming back together personally and professionally, which you can accommodate with various options. Building Camelot means redefining your workplace so everyone can feel safe and confident in coming back the way that best suits them.

Employers need to get on board with flexibility because it is here to stay, and people want more of it. Part of building your community will be defining flexibility with a discussion around fairness. Empower your people to choose their own level of flexibility in light of what's fair to everyone else. Let them come up with personal solutions versus getting stuck in the old model of command and control, where management made all decisions.

As we move back to work postpandemic, I am seeing our work cultures retreat into old behaviors. We are going backward because we are scared, and fear creates command and control. This is when we fall into the trap of saying, "I am going to tell you how it is going to be and do not ask questions." Acting from this place is a fast track to squashing innovation and pushing employees toward Posttraumatic Job Disorder.

Employees are your internal customers. As with external customers who you want to return and buy your products, you want employees to come back and show up for work eager to take on their day. If you pick up the hammer and say this is the one-and-only way things are going to be, people will withdraw from your workplace and start looking elsewhere. Instead, consider inviting or requesting them versus requiring them to engage the way they feel safest.

> **Your employees are experiencing you, but are you being purposeful about what *they* experience?**

Community is very much a mutual concept and experience. Ask your people what they want their community to look like, and they will tell you. I used to talk a lot about culture by design versus culture by default. Your employees are experiencing you, but are you being purposeful about what *they* experience? It is a subtle shift in thinking and a shift in how you engage with each other.

COMMUNITY ESSENTIALS

The key pillars for any community are simple. Communicate. Communicate. Communicate. Listen. Listen. Listen. It is crucial to embrace technology to communicate with your people. If it is not practical or appropriate to be together in person, just about everyone has discovered that video is a great way to connect with your employees for meetings.

I was at an event where forty people were attending in person and one attended online. Care was taken that everyone could see and hear that individual who, by the way, was the one person receiving an award. The thoughtfulness of the organizers obviously made him feel great—and very much included. I did not know why he couldn't be there; it didn't matter. He was happy. We are no longer living in an OR world; we are living in an AND world. Our communities need to reflect that.

Don't be afraid to use the technology of your choice to simply say, "I was thinking about your parents' visit over the weekend (or your daughter's soccer tournament), and I hope you had fun. You deserved the break." Communication of any sort is greatly appreciated by employees and is a meaningful way to show you are listening and you care.

Use technology to facilitate your community connections. Have an open house or a fireside chat to welcome your people into your home and connect on a deeper level. YouTube is one of the biggest social media channels, and it is being underused in building community within companies. Engage your internal customer the way they want to be engaged.

Think about creating messages to communicate with your employees on a platform they already know and love. Create unlisted videos and playlists to showcase messages or even a collection of silly videos for those times your people need a mental break. Look for ways to be creative and flexible using Instagram, Facebook, and snail mail to communicate.

COMMUNITY GUARDRAILS

Whether your employees are on-site, virtual, or hybrid, they need guardrails to define their flexibility, fairness, and community. How will meetings take place? Will everyone use a virtual background to feel mutually connected or would it be better to go natural, with no backgrounds so people get to know more about one another? What guardrails are needed for who speaks and when during meetings? Will there be a place and time for general social chatting like you normally have in the office before or after a meeting? Be clear and meet the needs of your team.

> **Whether your employees are on-site, virtual, or hybrid, they need guardrails to define their flexibility, fairness, and community.**

Consider the size of your groups and meetings. In big groups, people tend to shut down and not engage, especially your introverts. Divide into microgroups or use breakout room features in meeting software to make sure everyone is able to participate comfortably. Be thoughtful about how you hold meetings as well. Not everyone is comfortable with how they look on video; the background of their home office might embarrass them; they may fear family interruptions; or they could be very private and not want to share their home with everyone.

CREATE COMMUNITY HUBS

My team loves the shared office spaces we lease through Office Evolution. I love using them also when I travel. If my team wants to meet in South Carolina, they use the offices there. Have a group that wants to connect in Atlanta? We secure a shared office space or, if needed, a conference room or ballroom at a hotel. I highly recommend shared office spaces to foster community if workers cannot come into the office or are spread out across the country, not only do your employees get to have community with their coworkers but they can form a community in the office space they share temporarily with other workers in the same situation.

Businesses with large spaces are also getting creative and can accommodate guidelines for the safety and comfort of employees with individual tables, chairs, and spacing. Let people have their own safe space where they feel good about coming back together. I've had a virtual community at my company for eighteen years, long before it was sexy. When I was a new leader, I had a rigid schedule. I remember being irritated having thirty minutes of my agenda eaten up during the day by social chitchat in virtual meetings. But I realized how important this piece of the puzzle was. We were creating a remote culture of connectedness.

Do not lose touch with your people. Consistency is key in enabling your people to count on you. In my company, we have all our monthly meetings scheduled out for six months and then we discuss everyone's schedules for the best dates and times for the next six months. We blend flexibility and fairness with this pattern.

If you do not provide a good employee experience, you cannot compete for the best talent. Too many leaders are completely out of touch with what their employees need and do not know what they need themselves. People are exhausted. We are burned out because we are running lean and mean. We cannot help but wait for the next shoe to drop as we live in a constant state of hypervigilance and stress. These feelings are shared by everyone in your company's community, and this shared experience is critical for today's and tomorrow's sustainability.

Put your people first. Model the behavior you want to see. Show genuine interest and care. And you have created a Camelot Community.

Put your people first. Model the behavior you want to see. Show genuine interest and care.

Communities Are Not Born— Here's How They Grow

- Realize your company is a unique community, with shared relationships, trust, and common values.

- To get clear about what your people want and need—ask them.

- The command-and-control cultures of the past have created "posttraumatic job disorder," making people scared of returning to work.

- Treat employees with respect and empathy and communicate with transparency.

- Flexibility is here to stay; employees demand it, and you need to provide it.

- Whether they are on-site or virtual, employees need guardrails to define their flexibility, fairness, and community.

- Maximize opportunities for connections with shared workspaces, microgroups, and space for social connections.

- Put your people first.

Reflection & Notes

As people return to work, what are you doing, specifically, to ensure you're building an inclusive community for the mix of on-site, remote, and hybrid employees you have now? What measures are you taking to listen to your employees' experience in this new world of work? How will you maintain the flexibility you need to respond to ongoing change?

CONCLUSION

The four chapters in this book build on each other. Following this journey of instilling and giving trust, creating an incredible employee experience that supports the whole person, and authentically showing up and caring helps develop a community where your employees and your business can flourish. In a word, Camelot!

When you decide to run a business and hire people, you have decided to build a community focused on a common purpose. As an owner or a leader, you have a responsibility to both your people and their families. It may be hard to hold true to that commitment when things are constantly changing, but we have to accept the fact that change is our reality. It requires new understanding and different responses. This book is meant to be your guide.

The overall theme of this book is "put your people first." That means listening, respecting, inspiring, stepping away from judging, and giving people the flexibility and support to be the best versions of themselves. You'll see remarkable things happen when you put people first. I guarantee you'll get much more than you give and have more success!

This book represents the theory I have based my business model on and teach to my clients. It has worked through the Great Recession and through the pandemic as well as before and in between them. I invite you to follow my lead. In fact, I dare you to!

ACKNOWLEDGMENTS

I would like to thank my team of talented people at TalenTrust for inspiring me to be a better leader. Each of you teach me how to lead with empathy every day. Also, a big shout-out to Rachel Wadsley and Sherry Law who assisted greatly in the production of this book!

ABOUT THE AUTHOR

Kathleen Quinn Votaw is the CEO of TalenTrust, a strategic recruiting and human capital consulting firm that has helped companies nationwide address immediate needs and drive long-term growth since 2003. She is the author of *Solve the People Puzzle* and a key disruptor in her industry with a mission to help employers create people-centric, relationship-based workplaces.

She has helped more than one thousand companies across multiple industries navigate uncertainty and continuous change to develop purpose-based, inclusive cultures that inspire employees to come to work each day. A lifelong learner, Kathleen recently completed a Stanford Graduate School of Business program focused on strategy, innovation, and organizational design. She has also received numerous awards over her career including the coveted Inc. 5000.

Kathleen believes that when you build your business relationships on a foundation of kindness and love, all else follows. She teaches business leaders how to put people first by focusing on the employee experience as much as they focus on the customer experience to find the sweet spot of success. In this book, she helps employers and employees navigate the new way to work—from home, or anywhere, together.